DEDICATION

It's an Honor to write this book in memory of my late mother, Hope Anita Whiting.

Sharing priceless moments of her commitment to being a great mother and her inspiration.

My mother inspired me to trust and believe in God, no matter what obstacles or situations come your way. I Love You Mama!

INTRODUCTION

God and my mother inspired me to write this book in my 45 years of living. I have seen how God has provided, protected, pushed, and progressed me through life with the help and guidance of my mother.

Sometimes I wanted to give up and didn't want anything out of life. All I wanted to do was to go to work, drink on the weekends, and smoke weed. But God and my mother were a perfect tag team! They were the ones who would lift me up, encourage me, and help me get back on track, so I could become the man God wanted me to be!

In this book, I want to share some of the moments, struggles, and successes from my life. God and my mother have given me hope to pursue life relentlessly!

My mother's name is Hope, and she lived up to her name. She was the one who always encouraged me and others. God truly gave me **"Hope and a Future".** *(Jeremiah 29:11)*

CHAPTER 1
DON'T RUN FROM NOTHING OR NOBODY!

One summer afternoon, I went to play basketball at the court in my neighborhood in Parkview in Portsmouth, VA. I was around 14-15 years old and was pretty good, but I was still learning and trying to be the best.

I dreamt of playing basketball in college and possibly in the NBA. I would go to the court and get picked to play 5-on-5, full-court. As a kid with dreams of playing professional basketball, it meant a lot.

I remember thinking, "I am about to skin these cats up; they can't see me! I have been working on my jumper and ball-handling skills, aka my handles!" I'm like yeah, let's go!!!

We started playing, I was doing my thing, making my shots, blowing past the guys who were checking me, and talking trash! I was balling!! I made a shot, and during the trash-talking talking I said something.

Next thing you know, I was arguing with one of the guys. Now, trash-talking on the court can get intense in the hood. When someone gets in your face, you hit hard first. So I stole on him, and he hit me back, then I put him in a headlock.

All of a sudden, I got hit and kicked in the side by another kid. I knew I was about to get jumped, so I ran home as fast as I could. I got in the house, told my dad and mama what happened, that I was about to get jumped by two boys.

My mom didn't play! I saw her putting on her tennis shoes and asked, "Mamma, what are you doing?" She told me she was going to look for the two boys and talk to their mothers. No one was going to hurt her baby!

I tried to stop her, she asked me if I knew where they lived, I said no, thinking it would slow her down, but she said she would find them, and flew right out the front door looking for them. I was so scared that I didn't even bother going with her.

My mom came back about two hours later, saying she had found out where one of the boys lived and spoken with his mom, who said, "There should not be any more problems."

I learned a lesson from my mother that day! Never run away from your issues, oppositions; deal with them head-on! I was so scared to go with my mother to handle the situation.

But I learned years later, by reading the Bible and spending time with God, that *"He has not given us the spirit of fear" (2 Timothy 1:7)*. My mother wasn't scared and God showed me by her actions that I don't have to be scared either when trials and tribulations come my way in life!

Deal with everything by faith, knowing that God will protect you and give you the right words to say to whomever you are talking to (Jeremiah 1:8-9). God used that moment to show me there is hope in any situation if we only trust in Him.

CHAPTER 2
I WILL LIFT YOU UP!

When I was a child, I had some days when I didn't believe in myself. Part of that was because of what a classmate in school said to me, or not comprehending and understanding the questions the teacher asked me about the lesson she was teaching.

I would give the wrong answers to the questions, and the teacher would address me in a way before the class that made me feel dumb, and everyone laughed at me. My dad was an alcoholic, and I remember the days coming home to him being drunk and saying some very hurtful things to me.

When I was 13 years old, I told my dad I wanted to play professional basketball in the NBA. He told me you are not going to NBA you might play in the Nigga Basketball Association but not the NBA where Jordan, Magic, and Isaiah Thomas play. His friends were around and started laughing.

That hurt me and made me feel really bad. He repeatedly did this for years, making me feel less than. I really couldn't understand it as I was growing up. I'm his son, why would he say such hurtful things to me, what did I do to deserve this!?

I realized, as I got older, that it was the alcohol. When he got drunk, he would say anything out of his mouth. Now let me say this, I love my dad, and he loves me.

My dad is a good man, and I fully understand he had his own personal issues. Also, I understand God allowed me to go through it for the necessary shaping and molding me into the man He has chosen me to be.

We can always count on God to lift us up when people and situations try to bring us down. The Lord will always encourage us through His word. *(Isaiah 41:13)*

Despite his verbal abuse and drunkenness, my mother would encourage me to be the best Michael Derrick Whiting that I can be! She used to make me say my name out loud for me to feel confident in who I am.

She used to tell me, "You are Michael Derrick Whiting; you can become whatever you put your mind to! Don't let anyone disrespect you, don't let anyone tell you what you can't do, and believe in yourself!"

Whenever I was having a bad day, I would always call on my mother and God. They always gave me a word of encouragement to lift me up! As my mother used to encourage me during my down times, she used to tell me how God would always lift her up when she felt down, defeated, and felt like giving up!

How she would pray and read the Bible and God would give her a word to keep pushing, and to keep on going!

I got saved when I grew older and started to form my relationship with God. Besides devotion, anytime I was going through something, I would read the Bible and pray.

One day, I felt so down and felt like giving up. Nothing was going my way. Whether it was going through hard times at work or the tough times in my marriage. I remember everything my mama would say to me about how she used to read and pray, and that is exactly what I did one particular day.

I came home and prayed, and then started reading the Word. God led me to a very familiar scripture, ***Philippians 4:13, "I can do all things through Christ that strengthens me."*** I have read this scripture many times, but when I read it that day, I felt so empowered!!

The word of God has given me so much life!! I felt like I was Pac-Man in the video game. I was running away from people, situations, and life.

When I got a good taste of God's word, it fueled me like a power pellet that Pac-Man eats to gain energy and confidence to pursue what has been chasing him.

Philippines 4:13 is one of my favorite Bible verses. No matter what, God will be with me to do whatever He has called me to do!

CHAPTER 3
HOW ARE WE GOING TO MAKE IT

I was 14 years old when my mother decided to leave my father. They couldn't get along; she was tired of him getting drunk, verbally abusing her, and the occasional physical abuse.

She decided to leave because she saw how it was affecting me. I would get into arguments with my dad to the point we would almost get into fistfights because I didn't like how he was treating my mother.

She wanted to get me away from the chaos, and also, my mom had just given birth to my little brother. And she did not want him to go through any of the mess that I had experienced with her and my dad.

So, my mom sat me down one day and explained to me that she had decided to leave my dad and that my brother and I were going to have to stay with my grandparents in Gates County N.C for a couple of months until she found a place for us to stay.

In my mind, I was like good, I'm glad she is leaving my dad, even though I loved him, it was the right thing to do, also I wanted my mom to be happy, she deserved it! She wasn't perfect, but she was a great woman and a great mother! Many thoughts ran through my head about whether my mom leaves my dad, like, how is she going to take care of herself and two kids? How are we going to make it?

My dad was the breadwinner of the house, and my mom just worked part-time at the time. I knew money was tight and immediately thought, what if we have to move to one of the projects like Swanson Homes, JW, Lincoln Park, Ida Barber, or Dale Homes? I asked my mom if we were going to move to the projects, and she looked me dead in my eyes and said, "NO,

I am going to make sure you and your brother stay in a safe environment. I just want you and your brother to focus on school and stay out of trouble, I will handle the rest!"

My mother meant what she said. My brother and I stayed with our grandparents for a couple of months. Months later, she asked my granddaddy to bring me back to Portsmouth because she had found us a place to stay.

Our new home was a new apartment complex called Kingman Heights. When we got there, I was like, ok, Mama, you got us in a nice spot! Not only was it a nice spot as we were moving in, but I ran into one of my friends who stayed in my old neighborhood, my homeboy, Dontae.

There were some other friends I knew from school, Junior & Dominic, who lived out there too. I was excited because I was in a neighborhood where I already knew people I could play basketball and hang out with.

After staying at our new home for several months, I noticed how things were very limited.

There was not a lot of food or sweets in the house. I like oatmeal cookies, pies, and ice cream sandwiches in the freezer. There was only one box of cereal, and that was the one I couldn't stand, the Cheerios without the sugar! You know what I am talking about!

What kid liked the Cheerios without sugar? My mom used to get on me about wasting food and making sure I turned off the lights in the bedroom if I was not in there.

When she bought some groceries, she told me not to eat up everything, because the food had to last us for a month! I saw how things were tight, and I knew how it would be. I adjusted to the change, but what really frustrated me was not having cable TV!

During basketball season, I had to watch Michael Jordan and the Chicago Bulls! I used to go around my friend Junior's house every time the Bulls played because he liked Scottie Pippen.

Even though I adjusted very well, I saw how it was wearing my mother down. She was raising two kids by herself and trying to get back and forth to work, without a car. Going through different issues at her job and no personal life. She was trying her best to pay the bills and take care of her two boys.

I helped my mama as much as possible, I babysat my little brother, and I stayed out of trouble in school and at home. I did not want to put any extra stress on my mama. I used to hear her go to the bathroom and run the hot bath and hear her praying to God for help, then she would go to bed and cry herself to sleep.

My mom would wake up the next day right back at it again, working and coming home. Every day when my mom came home from work and after walking through the door, she would say, Lord, thank You!!

Despite what kind of day she had, all the stuff she had to put up with at work, and the two buses she had to catch to get home, no matter if it was cold or rainy outside, she would always say Lord, thank You!! She said Lil Mike, God got me through another day!!

As I grew up and started working, paying bills, and dealing with everyday life, I understood what my mother said. It's the Lord who will give you strength, He will provide, He will give you peace, He will make a way out of no way!!!

I watched God bless my mother to care for her kids while barely making over minimum wage. Nothing got cut off, and we ate a decent meal every day. God did what He said He would do, **Philippians 4:19, "I will supply all your needs according to His riches and glory."**

Just Know God Will Come Through When It Seems Like You Can't Make It Through! Just have Faith, the size of a mustard seed.
Matthew 17:20

CHAPTER 4
THE MOMENT THAT CHANGED MY LIFE

On July 7, 2001, I decided to go to Virginia Beach with one of my home boys and two of his friends to smoke some weed and drink three cases of my favorite beer at the time, Corona.

My mom begged me not to go and told me to stay home with my daughter Lenae, who was 5 years old at the time. I told her I wouldn't leave until I put her to sleep and asked if she would watch her for me.

After nagging her and convincing her that I would be all right, she said ok. As I'm on my way to Virginia Beach, about 40 minutes from my house,

I was speeding on the interstate, driving about 70 mph, moving from lane to lane, just showing off. Telling everyone in the car with me that I am a NASCAR driver and I got skills.

Then all of a sudden, my friend who was sitting on the passenger side grabbed my steering wheel, playing and said, "You don't got no skills." I instantly lost control of the car, the car started flipping like the cars in the movie, "Bad Boys 2".

My Toyota Tercel flipped about 4 times. The last time it flipped back on the wheels and hit the side wall on the interstate. By God's grace and mercy, my car didn't hit any other cars, hurting innocent people.

God's hand was on the four of us that evening; nobody got seriously hurt, and everyone walked away from the accident except for me. I had a really bad headache and a slight concussion.

When the ambulance came, they put me on the stretcher, and before they took me away, the officer asked if I had any guns or drugs in the car. I told him I had some weed and some beer.

He came back and told me that he found the weed, but said, "Don't worry about it!" That was the end of that, Thank God.

My mother arrived at the hospital not too long after I did. They allowed her to come see me after I was settled in my hospital room. We had a conversation that I will never forget.

She asked me when I was going to stop running the streets and focus on what I was going to do in life.I remember looking at her while she was talking and seeing how hurt she was.

After she got through talking, she left crying like someone had died. I started crying myself and praying to God, telling Him that when He gets me out of this, I promise I will give my life to Him, and surrender!!

I'm tired of running the streets, I'm tired of running from Him, and I don't ever want to see my mama cry like that again behind something I did!

Then I started thanking God for giving me a Second Chance. That accident should have killed me, but all I got was a really bad headache and a small cut on my left arm! I recognize that God had given up on me and He has given me Hope!!!!!

Even when things go wrong in your life, God will flip that situation over for your good!
Romans 8:28

CHAPTER 5
IT'S TIME

Once I got out of the hospital, I had made up my mind that I was going to change. First stop running the streets, living recklessly, and sleeping with multiple women.

Things needed to change, and I kept thinking about my car and how I survived, and how it made my mama feel seeing me laid up in the hospital. I prayed and told God I give up, I'm coming to serve Him, help me!

The same day I came home from the hospital, I had gotten a phone call from a female who I was trying to date. She asked me how I was doing and said she hadn't heard from me in a long time. I was like, girl, I just got out of the hospital, I was in a car accident.

She was in shock and asked me for my address and came to see me, we talked and she stayed in touch. We started dating months later.

One Sunday, I went to church with her at St. John Baptist Church in Portsmouth, VA. I hadn't been to church in a long time, it felt good getting dressed up and listening to old hymn songs I heard when I was a child, and hearing a word from the Lord!

As I was sitting there listening to the preacher, I felt in my spirit and my heart, God telling me, It's time!

God reminded me of how He spared me and showed mercy on me in my car accident and that I promised Him I would surrender and follow Him. I immediately started crying, and I said to myself, yep, it's time!

The pastor gave the invitation and asked if there was anyone who wanted to give their life to Christ?

That was my moment, and without hesitation, I got up and walked towards the altar. I made the best decision of my life, I gave my life to Christ!

I had such a big smile on my face because I knew I had done something great, as flashes went through my mind, all the stuff I had been through, my childhood, growing up in the church at First Baptist on Elm Avenue and Third Baptist.

I just felt a burden lifted off of me, I was full of joy!! The devil thought I was going down, but God lifted me up!!! God has given me life! I'm ready to move forward!!!!! When you give life back to Christ, you feel renewed, knowing you have a bright future ahead of you! *Joshua 1:9*

CHAPTER 6
GOD CALLED ME!

There is nothing like knowing you are on the right track and going in the right direction. Mike, you are now living for Christ and have made some adjustments in your life. You have proposed to your girlfriend(Kesha), and she said yes, and y'all are scheduled to get married in November.

My thoughts were exactly that, having the real talk with myself, and everything was going great, then something happened. One night, as I was sleeping, I had a dream. In the dream, I was lying face down on the ground. I wasn't dead, I was just lying there. Then a man stood right in front of me, and I just shot straight up!

 I didn't get up on my own, I just shot straight up! The man looked me straight in my eyes. His eyes were so bright, he had brown skin and was wearing a white and gold robe. Suddenly, I started mumbling real fast.

I realized later I was talking in tongues. Then the man turned me around, I stopped mumbling, and turned around to look for him. I couldn't find him. I saw these stairs going all the way up in the sky, and there he was standing on top of the stairway, then he disappeared, and I started yelling Jesus, Jesus!

My alarm clock went off then I woke up. I sat on the side of the bed in total shock. This dream was not my average dream, it was in another dimension. I knew I just had an encounter with God! I sat on the edge of the bed for about 10 minutes, then I finally got myself together and got ready for work.

I cried all the way to work thinking about what happened. When I got to work, I pulled one of my friends, Deacon Parker, to the side, who was saved and knew the word of God pretty well.

I told him about my dream which was out of this world! I needed answers, I'm hoping he could help me! He listened intently to everything I said, then he looked at me straight in the face and said, Mike, this doesn't happen to everyone.

He told me what to do: pray and ask God what He meant by the dream, then read His word, read the Bible, and do it repeatedly until you get an answer. I did exactly what he said, to pray and ask God what the dream meant, and read the Bible. I did this for several weeks, no answer!

Then one day, I came home from work and started reading. I came across **Genesis 28** when Jacob had a dream, and he saw God on top of a stairway. When I read this, it blew my mind! I couldn't believe what I just read in the Bible was what I saw in my dream! I went into the bathroom and started crying, and said I knew it was you in the dream, but what did you mean by it?

So I continued the process, I prayed and read for weeks and months went by, and no answer. One day, I was at work and went into the bathroom with my pocket Bible to read a chapter or two.

God led me to **Acts 26 16-18. The scripture says, "But arise, stand upon your feet, for I appeared to you for this purpose. To make thee a minister and a witness both of these things which thou hast seen, and those things in which I will appear unto thee.**

Verse 17 Delivering thee from the people and from the Gentiles, unto whom now I send thee, verse 18 To open their eyes, and turn them from darkness to light and from Satan unto God, that they may receive forgiveness of sins, and inheritance among them which are sanctified by faith that is in me."

Once I read this, I couldn't believe it. This is what I dreamt, and it's in the Bible. I read it again, then I said to God, I know you are not calling me to preach. Sure enough, that's exactly what He was doing. He had given me confirmation through a guest preacher who came to St. John Baptist.

God brought back to remembrance that two years prior, I had gone to Magic City with some friends, and a stripper stopped and looked at me and said You are a preacher, you are a pastor.

I said you must think I am someone else, my name is Michael Whiting. Then she said it again, You are a preacher, a pastor! I looked at my friend Eric and said, "This chick is crazy."

I didn't know at the time, but God used her to confirm what He was doing in my life.

I never dreamt or even thought of being a preacher. I always wanted to play in the NBA, but God had something else in mind. God called me to be a preacher/pastor, but I didn't see myself doing it. I looked at my past and the things I used to do.

I didn't feel like I was qualified. But the Bible says, **"that He knew you before you were formed in your mother's womb, Jeremiah 1:5."**

God already knew me and what I was going to do, and knew how things were going to turn out. God was working on me the whole time, and I didn't realize it. Now I tell everyone, ask God what your purpose is. Because who you want to be may not be who God has called you to be!

CHAPTER 7
WORDS THAT SCAR YOU!
WORDS THAT HEAL YOU!

Being called by God is an honor and a big responsibility. It's always an honor when the King of kings calls you to do anything for Him.

He believes in you, and He could have called someone else. Also, it's a sin not to do what you know He has called you to do. But if He calls you to do something, He will give you everything you need to complete the assignment.

God used certain individuals to help me on my journey to becoming a pastor. One was Pastor Gregory Thomas. He literally took me under his wing and taught me about ministry, pastoring, etc. I was attending two services every Sunday.

I would attend the first service at my home church and then immediately go to Pastor Thomas' church for their morning service. I highly appreciate the time and wisdom he poured into me.

I know God used him to encourage me because there were times others who were close to me didn't believe in me, and neither did I believe in myself. I had a conversation with someone I highly respected and looked up to.

They pretty much told me in so many words that I wasn't good enough to be a preacher. They said and did things that I will never forget. The things they said most definitely left a scar on me.

After I had this conversation with them, I felt sad and depressed. I was thinking about giving up! I was driving home, saying to myself, maybe they are right, that's why I keep going around in circles!

Then God immediately started talking to me! God said they didn't call you, I did!!! God showed me in the spirit all the times he had used me to preach at different churches and I wasn't even licensed. God also showed me people that I have encouraged to get saved.

Then God gave me my favorite scripture, **"I can do all things through Christ who strengthens me."** I just started crying, praising, and thanking Him!! The next day put the icing on the cake.

I went around my mother's house to tell her about the conversation I had with this person, and I told her everything that was said.

I will never forget what she said to me! We were in the kitchen, and she was cooking at the time. She slammed the spoon down, and said I don't give a beep beep what they said, you do what GOD called you to do.

My mother encouraged me to stay focused and reminded me that I am Michael Derrick Whiting and God is going to do great things through me! I felt so confident and eager to continue doing what God called me to do. I knew my mama was going to tell me the truth and lift me up!

As I was driving home, a song by LL Cool J came on, Mama Said Knock You Out! I was like WOW!! This song is about how his grandmother encouraged him not to listen to the critics and knock them out!

I thank God again, I told Him I'm going to stay focused and stay the course! God and my mama have been in my corner from day one! They have never let me down! When I was at my lowest, they were the two that consistently loved me, encouraged me, comforted me, and believed in me! GOD and my Mama raised me to be great!

That is exactly what I am going to do, BE GREAT! I will never forget when I asked my mama if she knew I was going to be a pastor/preacher when I was growing up. She told me something that changed my life! She said, "No, I did not know what you would become, but I knew you would be an upright man! I knew you were going to be righteous, because that's the kind of heart that you had! You always tried to do what was right!"

That blew my mind for days! You can be a successful lawyer, doctor, teacher, or even a preacher, but that does not mean you are going to be upright and honest.

That is when I remembered what she would always tell me, "No matter what someone else does, you always do what's right." **And a good name is better than all the riches in the world!!! (Proverbs 22:1)**

I love you, Mama! R.I.P.! God, I love you more than anything, thank you!! As Nipsey Hussle would say, "This is a Victory Lap!" I already have the Victory through Christ Jesus!

As long as we stay connected to God, He will make sure we will overcome any obstacle, disregard anyone who says or does anything that comes against His will for our lives! Trust Him! Victory is already yours!

CHAPTER 8
MY MAMA WASN'T PLAYING!

One night, I was hanging out with my friends, Dontae, Fraji, Antonio, and a few others. Fraji, was the one at the time who kept liquor in his trunk. Anytime you wanted a shot of whatever, he had it. That night we got so drunk, drinking beer and liquor.

We all ended up at my momma's house, where I was staying at the time. Usually after 9:00 pm, my mom is in bed and she wouldn't get up until the next morning.

My friend Dontae fell in the bathtub while using the bathroom. He fell so hard it woke my mama up out of her sleep. She came flying out of the bedroom and asked what was that noise?

I was afraid to say anything because I was drunk and I didn't want my mother to embarrass me. But I had to say something because she looked directly at me, wanting to know what was wrong!

I said Dontae fell in the tub and bumped his head and before I could finish, she said, "y'all been drinking, y'all are drunk." She immediately told me, Dontae, Fraji, and Antonio to give her our car keys, and told us we are not going no beep beep where! She said, "Call your girlfriend, your mama, whoever you need to call and tell them you are not coming home tonight."

All my friends did exactly what she said with no fuss. we all found a spot in the living room and went to sleep. We all woke up early the next morning laughing at each other and getting on Dontae on how he fell in the bathtub.

Then all of us said and admitted to one another that we were too drunk to go anywhere last night! We probably would have gotten DUI, went somewhere and got in some mess or would have accident and killed ourselves or somebody.

I made sure that I apologized to my mama for how we came into the house drunk like that. She looked at me and said, "Don't do that again!" Then she went on saying what could have happened if she hadn't woken up and stopped us. We would have gone to jail or would have been dead.

And she reminded me that I have family members on both sides of the family who are alcoholics, and if I don't watch myself, I would be just like them. I looked at her and she had a disappointed look on her face. Then I said Mama, you're right. I hugged her and said it won't happen again.

Later that day, after I got some rest, I thought about what happened and everything my mama said, and what could have happened if we had left the house and tried to drive somewhere else. I began to shake my head and thank God that we didn't go anywhere else.

My mama usually doesn't wake up out of her sleep, but that night God used my mama to make sure we didn't go anywhere! My mama saved us!

The old folks used to say God looks out for fools and babies! We weren't babies, we were most definitely the fools that night. I took my mama's words and ran with them, I haven't been drunk since.

I didn't like that look my mama had on her face. Also, I realized I didn't want to be drunk. Well, that was the end of that! Lesson Learned!

God would use people to check you when you are wrong. To help you recognize what you are doing is wrong. It is always good to have people around who don't want to see you go down the wrong path.

Pray that God will put people around you that is not scared to tell you the truth. The truth may hurt, but remember the truth is to help you.

CHAPTER 9
WHEN EVERYTHING HIT ME ALL AT ONCE

The year 2020 was rough! My mother passed away on February 24! She was my best friend, we talked to each other just about every day, sometimes twice a day.

A month before she passed, my second mother, Mrs. Jordan, had passed away, and I had the honor of doing her eulogy. Losing two powerful people in my life was rough, but moving forward into the year 2021.

I was still wrestling with losing my mother, and what was coming next was not what I expected. Around the month of June, I was having problems with my vision.

My eyesight would get blurry sometimes, and at times I couldn't read unless I really stared at it for a while. After realizing something was wrong, I knew I needed to go to an eye doctor and find out why I was having problems with my vision!

I went to the eye doctor, and after examining my eyes, he told me I have swelling behind my eyeballs, which is called Papilledema.

I asked the doctor, "What is Papilledema? I never heard of that before!" To make it simple, he told me that the swelling behind my eyeballs can cause me to go blind or die.

He also said that I need to admit myself to a hospital as soon as possible so they can run further tests and come up with a solution to treat it. I was blown away, I was like wow, ok and asked the Lord what was going on?

So I did exactly what the doctor told me. I checked myself into the hospital, and they ran several tests on me and got samples of my blood.

The testing took several days, but on the third day, about ten doctors came into my room with shocking news! They told me what the eye doctor had already told me about having Papilledema, the reason for my blurry vision, and it needed to be treated ASAP, or I could go blind or lose my life!

Then they told me I have kidney failure and that my kidneys are only functioning at 15 percent, and that very soon I will have to go on dialysis!

When I thought they were done telling me everything that was wrong with me, they saved the worst for last.

They said they saw abnormal growth on both my kidneys, and it could be cancer! I was in total shock; I couldn't believe all these things were wrong with me at one time!

The doctors said, "We know this is a whole lot at one time, but we have a plan to deal with each issue." At that time, I didn't hear anything they were saying, I just couldn't believe it. I was scared and thought I was going to die, just a lot of things were going through my mind!

The next day, my wife had to explain to me everything the doctors had said. To help me understand that everything is going to be alright, that God has me, and that I have to go through the process of having surgery and getting healed.

I started praying and asking God to strengthen me and increase my faith to go through this process! Because there was no way possible I was going to make it without Him! The Lord instantly encouraged me! He told me I will get through this, I will not die.

Gradually, I took my mind off what I was going through and had my focus on God.

My God can not lie, He told me,

"I can do ALL things through Christ who strengthens me." (Philippians 4:13) My God said, ***"by His stripes I am healed!" (Isaiah 53:5).***

God let me know that everything was in His hands, He got this! I received everything that the Lord was saying to me, the Lord had given me hope, and everything was going to be alright!

God reminded me of how I survived my car accident back in 2001! It was He who kept me alive!

My car flipped four times on the interstate, and the only thing I had was a headache and a scratch on my arm. I began to thank God and knowing that God was going to take care of me!

1 Peter 5:7, "Cast all your anxieties on Him because He cares for you."

Jesus loves and cares for us, we should carry all of our burdens to Him. Whether you are going through a divorce, looking for a job, having a hard time getting along with your child, whatever it is give it ALL to God!

There is nothing that He can't handle. God loves all of His children. Just put everything in His hands. Watch everything will work out for your good.

CHAPTER 10
THE HEALING BEGINS

I had to have surgery where they were going to remove both of my kidneys due to kidney failure and the cancer that was on both kidneys. When the doctor told me they had to remove both kidneys because there was a chance that the cancer might spread, I was shocked and confused!

I was wondering how in the world can I live if both of my kidneys are gone! He explained to me that it had to be done, my kidneys were working at 15 percent, and that the cancer might spread if I didn't have the surgery. Also, this will help me get a transplant a lot quicker.

He said I would not be able to get a transplant if I have cancer in my body, also by removing both kidneys, there is a lower chance that the cancer will come back.

Even though it sounded like a good plan, I still couldn't get over what he said about removing both of my kidneys.

He saw the confusion on my face. He said, "Mr. Whiting, go home and think about it. You and your wife talk about it, and let me know what you want to do next week."

My wife, Kesha, and I discussed it; she thought I should follow the doctor's advice and trust the process. My mind was so wrapped around me having no kidneys, and part of me didn't want to go through this surgery because I was scared!

So, I did some research to see if anyone else had experienced the same thing and if there was another way to get around this. In my research, I asked other doctors what the best way to deal with my situation.

From all the information and listening to different doctors, it all led to one thing: I had to have the surgery and start the process of getting a transplant.

Wow! I still was not convinced totally, like I said, part of me was scared to have this surgery, I didn't want to be put to sleep for a long time, what if something goes wrong and I don't wake up?

A lot of things were going through my head! Then God started speaking to me! He said, **"I have not given you the spirit of fear."** *(2 Timothy 1:7)*. I prayed to God, told him how I felt, and asked for help through this process.

God told me to go through with the surgery, have faith and trust in Him that he will get me through it. I felt a whole lot better, but God wasn't finished.

I called my cousin Denise and talked to her about everything I was going through and God used her to speak to me and remind me how great God is!

Denise shared with me that she has had multiple surgeries and how God got her through them all, and some things to look for when I go through this process! She said Lil Mike, "you got this, and your faith in God will get you through this!"

My conversation with my cousin was very encouraging as she talked about some of the things she is going through, her belief in God, and having faith, knowing God will come through on her behalf.

When I got through talking to her, that was the icing on the cake, I was ready to go through the procedure of having this surgery.

I praised God for giving me a word of encouragement and strength! God said, **"that He will never leave us or forsake us." (Deuteronomy 31:6)**

It felt so good to hear from God, with Him letting me know that He will be with me every step of the way! A week later, at my doctor's appointment, I told the doctor, "Let's do this, I'm ready!" He said, "Ok, I'm ready too, and I will get a phone call letting me know when, where, and everything I need to do before the surgery."

Man! I felt so relieved! I went from being confused and scared to being excited about going under the knife and getting this cancer out of my body by removing both of my kidneys. God is awesome! I like how He will help and comfort you in the time of need!

Amid your confusion and doubt, God will give you peace and confidence, letting us know that He will never leave us or forsake us and that He is in control, if we just trust and believe in Him. In sickness, **"by his stripes we are healed." (Isaiah 53:5)** We have to believe that God will come through.

CHAPTER 11
YOU HAVE NOT BECAUSE YOU ASK NOT

Well, I had my surgery, and it was a success! They removed both of my kidneys, and now I am cancer-free! I was so happy that part was over with. I was also so happy that they caught the cancer, and it didn't spread.

It was a five-and-a-half-hour surgery. I stayed in the hospital for three days to make sure there were no complications. As I was sitting in the hospital bed, all I could do was thank God and think about getting a kidney transplant.

I asked some of my family members if they could think about being a potential donor, but most of them denied me.

I must admit, I was hurt because I felt like we were close, and there was no way they would deny me and let me go out like that, especially when they knew this was a life and death situation.

They told me their reasons, I accepted it, but was still disappointed. However, there were other family members I didn't ask who were willing to donate their kidney to me. God knows how to work things out, even though it seems like it doesn't look good.

An unexpected breakthrough happens. I get home from the hospital, still praising and thanking God for getting me through the surgery and being cancer-free. The surgery builds up my faith, now I'm ready to get a transplant!

One day, my wife and I were talking about getting a transplant. She was committed to donating her kidney if she was a match, she came up with an idea. She said, "Why don't you tell people what you are going through, and maybe someone will be willing to donate their kidney to you."

I was totally against it, I didn't want to tell the world my business and what I was going through. In my mind, nobody cared about me or what I was going through; nobody wanted to help me on that level. Even though I was against it, a part of me was thinking about it.

I had a conversation with my cousin Pam and told her the idea my wife came up with, making what I'm going through public and putting it on social media. Pam agreed with my wife and said something that helped me understand this will help and bless me.

Pam said, "How can people help you if they don't know what's wrong with you?" Something just clicked in my mind and spirit, I told Pam that they were right!

I'm going to make this public and trust God that everything will be alright. Later that week, after talking with my wife and cousin Pam, I decided to share my situation publicly on Facebook and TikTok.

Once I put it out there about having both kidneys removed and going through dialysis three times a week, people on Facebook started reaching out to me, saying they were praying for me.

Others asked if they could do something to help me, and some wanted to donate their kidney. This brought me so much hope and joy. I didn't know so many people loved and cared about me!

It's been times I felt alone. I knew I had God and my wife Kesha, but I wanted that support. I must say God put family, church family, and friends around me who really cared!

I got a call from a local news broadcaster that wanted to do a story on me about having my kidneys removed, going through dialysis, and looking for kidney donors. I was amazed and said, "Yes, I would love for you to interview me."

We did the interview, and everything went great. Many people called me and reached out to me, saying I really inspired them and that my faith in God is a blessing for them.

It was good to hear that what I was going through was helping someone else in what they are going through.

As I waited to get a kidney transplant, God was always with me. He has given me strength when I felt like giving up.

Getting tired of getting two needles stuck in my arm three times a week. At times after dialysis, I would feel so weak I would come home and sleep until the next day.

There were times I would be so weak after dialysis that I would fall asleep in the parking lot. One time, I came home after dialysis, pulled in the parking lot, and was so weak that I fell asleep again.

My wife, Kesha, looked out the window and saw me in the car, not moving, and thought I could have been on the phone. After being in the car for about ten minutes, she came to my car and found me asleep.

Kesha helped me in the house, and I went back to sleep, but at that moment I said, "Lord, I'm tired of this, it's draining me!"

Time had gone by, I was going through dialysis, hoping that sometime soon I would get a kidney! I'm glad I talked to someone about what I was experiencing and shared it on social media. We all need prayer and support from others.

The Bible says, ***"When two or three come together in His Name, He is in the midst." (Matthew 18:20).*** I praise God for His love and everyone who prayed and supported me! Thank you!

There were times I would be so weak after dialysis that I would fall asleep in the parking lot. One time, I came home after dialysis, pulled in the parking lot, and was so weak that I fell asleep again.

My wife, Kesha, looked out the window and saw me in the car, not moving, and thought I could have been on the phone. After being in the car for about ten minutes, she came to my car and found me asleep.

She helped me in the house, and I went back to sleep, but at that moment I said, "Lord I'm tired of this, it's draining me!" Time had gone by, I was going through dialysis, hoping sometime soon I would get a kidney!

CHAPTER 12
A BLESSING CAME BEFORE A BLESSING

My wife and I were married on November 30, 2002. That was one of the best days of my life. We were deeply in love and couldn't wait to get home from work and spend time together, especially on weekends when we were both off. We spent our quality time together and had a lot of fun on the weekends, you know what I mean!

One particular weekend, Kesha suggested we should buy a house and start looking at some around the 757. I thought, "Okay, let's do this! " We started looking and we saw several houses that we liked and continued our search the following weekend. Then we found a house of our interest.

We were approved for a loan for a certain amount, but not enough of what we were expecting. The bank advised us that if we pay off a couple more bills, we will get approved for the amount we wanted.

This is when I got scared! Kesha and I had not even been married a year yet. I felt like I wasn't making enough money to pay a mortgage. I was also paying child support at the time. I told my wife I didn't think it was the right time for us to buy a house.

We couldn't afford it. I wasn't making enough money, and with paying child support, there is no guarantee I can work overtime every week at the shipyard.

Kesha got upset and told me everything is going to be fine, stop being scared, you don't have any faith, she said, "We already got approved, the only thing you have to do is pay off some more debt, and we are in our new house."

Her speech didn't work, we kept going back in fourth for almost a month, then Kesha said the heck with it and left it alone.

In 2018, I couldn't wait to see the month of June, this is the year and month that my son will be graduating from high school, and my child support payments would end.

I planned to save enough money to get Kesha and me the house she has patiently waited for years! My son graduated. I was so proud of him and excited because the child support will be over. I will finally get a full check.

Around August of 2018, my mother and I had a conversation, and I told her about my vision of buying a brand-new house from the ground up. She immediately starts encouraging me, letting me know I can do it and God will bring it to pass.

Every other week, my mother reminded me of the vision of getting a house she didn't want me to lose hope, to keep on pushing, and not to give up! She encouraged me all the way to her death.

Four years later, in 2022, I was determined to get my family and I a house this time. I came across a friend of the family who was a realtor.

I saw a social media post stating they could help you get a house with a certain credit score. I instantly reached out to them about helping me get a house for my family.

We met with the realtor and her team and found a new development neighborhood where they were building new homes. They showed us a lot of new construction homes by the water. Immediately, one caught my attention! Kesha and I talked about it. I asked her if she liked the spot where our house could be built, and she said yes. we prayed for it right on the spot.

They told us how much the deposit would be to hold the lot, to build our future home. We agreed the process had begun. Kesha and I were so excited that what we had been praying for was coming to pass.

I thanked God and praised Him for all that He was doing! Watching the process of our house being built from the ground up was amazing! Just about every day, I went to watch them build our new home.

God let me know He heard my prayers and blesses those who believe in Him! Finally, the house was built, and it was time for closing.

On closing day will always be memorable for me. Kesha and I were on the way to our new home to sign the papers. Kesha held my hand, and she took her index finger and scratched the middle of my palm.

This really blew my mind because when I was a child, my mama used to hold my hand while we were walking around Tower Mall or Mid City in Portsmouth and scratched the middle of the palm of my hand and she told me that it meant I love you.

In that moment, it was like God was showing me that Mama was celebrating with Kesha and me on this great accomplishment. Even when she is no longer with me in the physical, she is here in the spirit.

It is always a great joy when God blesses us with things we prayed for and patiently waited for. God hears our prayers, but God always does things right on time.

Just keep the faith, knowing that God is going to come through for you! **Hebrews 11:1,**

"Faith is the substance of things hoped for and evidence of things not seen."

Don't give up on what you have been praying for because it's going to come.

CHAPTER 13
THE SECOND BLESSING

Kesha and I finally moved into our new house in August 2023. God blessed me and answered my prayers. This is another memory to add to my list.

A few months later, in November, Kesha and I had a housewarming party where family and friends came to celebrate and show their support.

During the celebration, I thanked everyone for coming and showing their support and talked about how God blessed Kesha and me with this house before my mama passed away.

She believed and encouraged me to get what I have been praying for, now God is going to bless me with a Kidney!

When I said it, I believed every word I said because if God blessed me with this house, He is going to bless me with a kidney!

On Saturday, June 15, 2024, that evening I went for a walk around the neighborhood, trying to get a little exercise in. After my walk, Kesha and I sat on the porch talking for about 15 minutes, then I got a phone call from UVA transplant.

When I saw their phone number, I hesitated to answer. I looked at Kesha with a silly look and said, "It's UVA!" She told me to answer the phone, and when I did, the UVA representative introduced herself.

She informed me that they had a kidney for me and proceeded to give me instructions and asked if I accepted the arrangements. She gave me five minutes to make a decision, and before I could answer, my wife said yes!

The UVA representative started laughing, then I said Yes, I accept.

The representative stated we had until midnight to arrive at the location, get checked in, and be prepped for surgery that would start around 5:30 am. I said ok, "I will be there", and hung up the phone. We started to get ready and drive to Charlottesville, VA.

As we were getting ready, I was in shock, thanking the Lord, and thinking, "This is really happening." I'm about to get a kidney! Wow, Lord, You Did It!

Things that I have been through on dialysis, times I was in pain about to pass on while I was on dialysis, I was back forth, in and out the hospital and times the devil tried to convince me to give up, you are going to die right here in Maryview hospital where your mom passed away at.

I cried while thanking God for keeping me strong when I was sick and weak, He did everything He said He was going to do! We finally got ourselves together and packed our clothes for at least two weeks.

When you are on the kidney transplant list, they tell you to have a bag packed so you will be ready when they call you. Hardhead, I didn't have a bag packed, but I'm so glad I didn't miss that phone call; I would have missed my blessing! We prayed, asking God to give us traveling mercy because we needed to be in Charlottesville by midnight.

We made it, 20 minutes late, but we made it. I checked in, they gave me a room, and went over everything they were going to do around 5:30-6:00 am. I went into surgery, and the six-hour surgery went well, A Success! I felt weak, but good! The doctors who performed the surgery came into my room and asked how I was feeling. They told me what I had to do and what to expect during my healing process.

To God be the Glory! We must wait on God; He will come through with a blessing when we least expect it. Trust and believe, and praise God while you are waiting on Him.

CHAPTER 14
FAMILY FRIENDS & CHURCH FAMILY

During my journey through Life, there have been people that God has used besides my mother who helped me through life's ups and downs. As a child, I had the best grandparents!

First, my Grandmother Kat was my father's mother. She was beautiful and funny at times (she could be a hot mess, don't judge my grandmamma), those who knew her know what I'm talking about.

She was the one who spoiled me and gave me the best Christmas I ever had as a child. She and my Uncle Kim gave me 40+ gifts and a bike, a beach cruiser, one Christmas.

My grandmama Kat said, "All these gifts are for you." I had Toys R US right in my grandma's living room!! I wish y'all could have seen my eyes, they are already big, but were five times bigger. I had plenty more Christmas moments like this before and after.

To give you a better understanding, I was her only grandchild for 15 years, before my brother Markus, cousins LJ and Kimberly, I had it going on!

My Grandmother gave me things my parents couldn't give me at the time, but the most important thing with her is the love and the time spent together.

Being with her was an outlet from other things I was dealing with as a child. Her picking me up every Friday was a blessing; God used her to help give me a better childhood. When I think about her, I start crying and thanking God for her. She was my Grandma, I love her, her crazy self.

Then it was my mother's parents, my grandparents Raleigh & Vivian Roberts. My grandfather was a quiet man who didn't take no mess. He was the one out of everyone in my family who would discipline me any time I did something wrong.

He was old school when it was time to discipline me, telling me to pull down my pants so he could whoop me. In this day and time, it would be child abuse, but I must admit this really helped me as a teenager going into adulthood.

I knew my grandfather wanted me to do what was right and stop with the mischievous things I was doing. Before you judge my granddaddy, let's go to the Word of God.

In the Bible, **Proverbs 23:13-14. NIV Do not withhold discipline from a child, if you punish them with the rod, they will not die. Verse 14: Punish them with the rod and save them from death.**

My Grandfather saved me. I grew up in Portsmouth, one of the toughest cities in Virginia. My Grandfather disciplined me at an early age, there will be consequences for every decision you make, and it trained me to make the right decision

His discipline helped me to stay out of trouble while I was helping my mother, who was raising two boys on her own. I didn't want to put any extra stress on my mother, she was already going through.

As an adult, it helped me as temptations come on a higher level, the discipline from Granddaddy helped me to turn away from a lot of unnecessary mess and drama by thinking of the punishment I'm going to have to face, jail or death if I go that way.

I thank God for the role my grandfather played a key role in my life. Then there was my grandmother, Sarah Vivian Roberts, who was funny and a hot mess, as well, in a joking way. Grandma Vivian cared for and loved all her grandchildren.

She cooked and cared for me, brought and ironed all of my clothes, and made sure I had everything I needed, as well as being sharp and clean for school.

God put me around some great-grandparents who loved, guided, and disciplined me as a child, helping me to make my life that much better. I love and thank them for that.

My father's brother, Kim aka UNC was a blessing to me growing up! Kim was my favorite uncle! He used to take me to every Wilson High School home football game at Frank D. Stadium in Portsmouth, VA. I would sit in the booth where he recorded the school football games, eating nachos and Reese's Peanut Butter Cups he bought for me.

I loved watching Wilson and Norcom High play each other. It seemed like the whole City of Portsmouth was there in the 80s and early 90s. Unc took me to his basketball games when he played in the church league at Third Baptist Church. I loved riding with him in his new white and tan Nissan, the nicest car I had ridden in at the time. Unc just was doing his unc duties chilling with his nephew.

I was his favorite nephew and went everywhere with him, including trips after he married his wife. I remember when they took me on their family vacation to Myrtle Beach, South Carolina. We visited different amusement parks and I had the best time with them at the beach. My uncle was my hero!

God used him to fill a void in my life as a young boy growing up needing every positive male figure to help me stay focused and not get lost in the streets.

A world where you can get caught up using drugs and hanging with the wrong people. He was a good example for me. I never told him how much I love him and am thankful for him being the best uncle a young boy could have.

I never told him this but hopefully, he will read this and know I really appreciate everything he has done for me!

I am the pastor of First Baptist Burdette in Franklin, VA, and God has blessed me with a wonderful church family, as well as The Mount Church Family, which spans all over the 757 area.

The members of both churches had been a blessing in so many ways. The FBBC and The Mount family prayed for me, encouraged and blessed my wife with anything we needed when I had both kidneys removed and my transplant.

During that time, I was out of work and didn't know how we were going to make it. For months, Kesha had to take time off from work with us traveling back and forth to the UVA hospital.

God says in **Philippians 4:19, "God Shall Supply All of Your Needs According to His Riches and Glory."** God did just that and more using the help of FBBC and the MOUNT family.

There have been friends who have helped me with prayer and their giving. One of my best friends, Keedy, was there through the good and the bad.

I knew Keedy since childhood, even though I was a couple of months older than he, I looked at him as my big brother.

If I had a problem, I needed someone to talk to or for advice, he was there. Keedy was the one who taught me how to dress when we were teenagers.

One day, we were on the school bus going home, and I had some pants that looked like something that Bruce Lee would wear in his movies.

Keedy started to joke on me and then he started to sing a song saying, "EVERYONE WENT KUNG-FU FIGHTING!"

Everyone on the bus who heard him started laughing. Even I fell out laughing as they would say, "he cooked you."

But when we got off the bus, he started giving me some advice on how to dress better, I appreciated his advice. To me, Keedy was before his time, very book smart and street smart.

I enjoyed the conversations we used to have about life and God. We used to talk about Jesus and scripture for hours.

Those conversations helped me in so many ways. And the prayers we had together really got us closer to God and gave us hope despite all the problems we shared.

We had been friends for thirty years before passing away in 2024. I thank God for blessing me with a big brother from another mother.

God also blessed me with my brothers and sisters on Social Media, also friends I have known for years, don't want to start naming everyone, don't want to forget them.

I want to thank a local news reporter from Wavy TV 10 who interviewed me when I had both my kidneys taken out. Thank you!

I am a witness, God and good people make the world a better place. God put people in place to help you and to make things happen.

CHAPTER 15
GOD BLESS WITH A HELP MEET

On November 30, 2002, I married the woman who has my heart, Kesha D. Johnson. I knew when I decided to get married, it was a big move for many reasons. One of the reasons is that my wife will be number 1 and not my mother. My mother has always been there and taken care of me.

Whether I was sick, hungry, needed advice, or someone to vent to, she was the one I would go to. Kesha and I are married, and she is now doing some of the things my mother used to do. She is cooking for me, taking care of me, she is the one I would vent to now.

Kesha has been a blessing to me. God used her in many ways and many times during our marriage. In February 2020, my mother passed. I was hurt, and my heart was broken.

While dealing with my mother's passing, I was also dealing with issues in my marriage. Kesha and I were on the verge of being separated and maybe divorced, but God had the Last Say So!

He touched both of our hearts and brought us back together. It brought joy to my heart because the devil tried to convince me there was no way you and Kesha could make it work. But God had given us hope!

We talked it out and concluded this is not what either one of us wanted. Getting to the heart of the situation, we realized it wasn't something to get a divorce.

At times, we praised God and cried because He kept us! I'm a man who really loves God, my family, and my wife is a big part of my family.

When my mama passed away, I was on dialysis and getting a kidney transplant, God used Kesha to keep me alive!

All this happened right behind each other. Praying to God to get me through this, don't let me die, there is so much I want to do. God answered my prayers, and I am forever thankful.

God kept Kesha and me together because He brought us together *(**Matthew 19:6**)*. God knew I couldn't deal without Him and Kesha.

Through Life with all trials and tribulations, the obstacles, the illness, the disappointments, the passing of loved ones, and more, God has shown me, **"He will never leave me or forsake me." (Deuteronomy 31:6) "By His stripes I am healed." (Isaiah 53:5)**

God gives me Hope in the midst of thinking this is it! I pray for anyone who reads this book that God will be with you if you just trust and believe. I am so proud to announce to the World I am a child of God and Can't NOBODY CAN DO YOU LIKE JESUS!

CHAPTER 16
TRUST HIM HE WILL COME THROUGH

Going through life, I have had good times and bad times. I don't know what's going on most of the time, but one thing is for sure: there is never a time that God hasn't been right there with me.

As I look back at my life, I see God was right there with me through it all. During the years, I have been saved, given my life to Christ, and have had a genuine relationship with Christ.

By spending time with God, I realize He loves me and all of His children. There is no greater love that we can receive from anybody more than Jesus. When I was at my lowest, I didn't believe in myself, and there was a time when I felt like I couldn't talk to or share my mistakes with anyone.

Who would not let me fall and laugh at me when I do. I'm here to testify that my Lord and Savior Jesus will not let us fall to the point where there is no return.

Jesus has gotten me out of some situations that I should have killed, but God. I will forever give Him glory. I was taught to always say thank you when someone does something for you.

God has done everything for me; that's why I always have a Thanksgiving Praise everywhere I go. Whether I'm in church, sitting at the red light, getting dressed, or buying groceries for the house, I realize all that I'm doing is because of the Lord.

Even when I have struggled to pay bills or things are not going my way, I still say thank you and I love you. I make it known to the world how grateful I am and how I love the Lord so much! Jesus is always showing His love to me.

At times, I know I'm doing wrong, and God forgives, blesses, provides, and protects me from my enemies and my own foolishness that will hurt myself and our relationship.

God expresses His love constantly to me, and I do my best to do the same. Recognizing the love God has for me gives me strength, confidence, faith, love, and hope.

When you truly recognize the love God has for you, you don't want to let it go. I want to be obedient; I want to love Him with all my heart, my soul, and strength, and my neighbor as I love myself.

Going through the ups and downs, and it feels like you work and you don't have anything to show for it. You can never go wrong in trusting in the Lord. It doesn't matter what you are going through.

You might be having problems with your children, family, relationships, with forgiveness, struggles in life, or on your job; I must give you the 411 just in case you didn't get it. The Lord Jesus Christ will turn around any situation you may be in when you faith and trust in Him.

God will give you hope when it seems like you are going to give up *(**Galatians 6:9**)*. God will send somebody you know or a stranger to provide with words of encouragement or get approvals for what you have been believing for just to let you know God has heard your prayers and to remind you, He will never leave you or forsake you.

The Lord loves His Children. He wants the best for us, but most of all, He wants us to stay connected to Him. The Lord doesn't want us to ever doubt Him.

He will make a way out of no way, even when it seems like things are not going to get any better. The only thing you have to do is pray and believe!

When they say prayer changes things they are telling nothing but the truth.

I have seen God bless, heal, and deliver people from prayer and having faith that He will do it. Trusting and having faith in God helps us to have a strong relationship with Him.

The bible says the only way to please God is by faith. Trusting in God is very important. We can always count on God. I have seen Him act on my behalf through the good and the bad.

My brothers and sisters, God will be there when no one else will. He will be right there for you *(Psalm 27:10)*. I will always say how good God is, no matter where I go or even on social media. He has healed, saved, and kept me in my right mind.

I am no longer the man of my past because of His goodness. He can change your life, too. I use my testimony of the things God has gotten me through to give them Hope!

I will always say how good God is, no matter where I go or even on social media. He has healed, saved, and kept me in my right mind. Because of His goodness, I am no longer the man of my past. He can change your life, too.

God has great things in store for you ***(Jeremiah 29:11).***

(Romans 15:13), My prayer for everyone who reads this book will get closer to God and will have an understanding that no one will ever love you more than Jesus, and there is always hope when you believe in Him.

God loves you, just believe that things are going to get better! Because **"God Has Given you Hope."**

www.ingramcontent.com/pod-product-compliance
Lightning Source LLC
Chambersburg PA
CBHW072203160426
43197CB00012B/2501